Presented to

Scarlett Marshall

by Kiltarlity Free Church

_2021_

The Lord be with you.
Ruth 2:4

KIDS READ TRUTH™
A companion to She Reads Truth™ and He Reads Truth™

Text and illustrations ©2018 by Kids Read Truth, LLC

Written and edited by Raechel Myers, Melanie Rainer, Russ Ramsey, and Amanda Bible Williams
Creative direction by Ryan Myers
Design and illustration by Trish Mahoney
Kid Consultants: Ellie, Etta, Hazel, Julian, Luca, and Oliver

Printed and bound in Nashville, Tennessee

3 4 5 6 7

ISBN: 978-1-946282-80-4

For bulk orders, contact orders@shereadstruth.com.
For additional products and information, visit kidsreadtruth.com.

This Is the
GOSPEL

A Kids Read Truth™ Story & Scripture Book

Illustrated by
TRISH MAHONEY

KIDS READ TRUTH

God made everything—
the planets and the stars,

the land and the water,

the animals and the plants.
**Everything was
made by God.**

Genesis 1:1   ¹ In the beginning God created the heavens and the earth.

And
EVERYTHING
GOD MADE WAS
GOOD.

⁹ Then God said, "Let the water under the sky be gathered into one place, and let the dry land appear." And it was so. ¹⁰ God called the dry land "earth," and the gathering of the water he called "seas." And God saw that it was good.

Genesis 1:9–10

Then God made

Adam & Eve,

the first people.
He made them in His image.
They lived with God
in the garden of Eden.

Genesis 1:27 27 So God created man in his own image; he created him in the image of God; he created them male and female.

God gave them
everything they needed.

[29] God also said, "Look, I have given you every seed-bearing plant on the surface of the entire earth and every tree whose fruit contains seed. This will be food for you…"

Genesis 1:29

God told them they could eat fruit
from any tree in the whole garden,

EXCEPT ONE.

[16] And the Lord God commanded the man, "You are free to eat from any tree of the garden, [17] but you must not eat from the tree of the knowledge of good and evil, for on the day you eat from it, you will certainly die."

Genesis 2:16–17

But an evil serpent lied to them,

and Adam and Eve **disobeyed God.**

They **sinned.**

Genesis 3:4,6

[4] "No! You will not die," the serpent said to the woman... [6] So she took some of its fruit and ate it; she also gave some to her husband, who was with her, and he ate it.

Because they sinned, Adam and Eve
could not live in the garden with God anymore.
God sent them away, and He told them
life would be very hard.

**But He still loved them
very much.**

23 So the Lord God sent him away from the garden of Eden to work the ground from
which he was taken. 24 He drove the man out and stationed the cherubim and the
flaming, whirling sword east of the garden of Eden to guard the way to the tree of life.

Genesis 3:23–24

**Because Adam sinned,
all people always would sin too.**

Romans 5:12 ¹² Therefore, just as sin entered the world through one man, and death through sin, in this way death spread to all people, because all sinned.

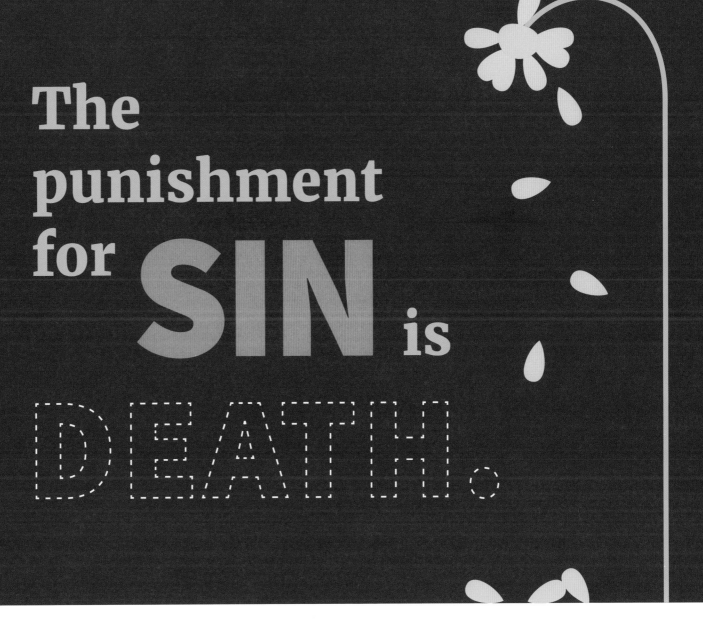

The punishment for **SIN** is DEATH.

23 For the wages of sin is death, but the gift of God is eternal life in Christ Jesus our Lord.

Romans 6:23

Sin affects the whole world.
God's good creation is now full of

fighting,
disappointment,
sickness,
and death.

Isaiah 24:4–5   [4] The earth mourns and withers; the world wastes away and withers; the exalted people of the earth waste away. [5] The earth is polluted by its inhabitants, for they have transgressed teachings, overstepped decrees, and broken the permanent covenant.

SIN separates us from God

because
GOD IS HOLY.

God can never sin.

[2] But your iniquities are separating you from your God, and your sins have hidden his face from you so that he does not listen.

Isaiah 59:2

But God loved His people very much.

He had a plan.

Jeremiah 31:3   [3] I have loved you with an everlasting love; therefore, I have continued to extend faithful love to you.

Someone
would have to take
the punishment for our sin.

And that
Someone
would have to live and not sin.

26 For this is the kind of high priest we need: holy, innocent, undefiled, separated from sinners, and exalted above the heavens.

Hebrews 7:26

So God sent His Son.
Jesus came to earth just like us, as a baby.

Matthew 1:21 21 She will give birth to a son, and you are to name him Jesus, because he will save his people from their sins.

Jesus taught people about God.
He loved people
and healed them.

Matthew 15:29–31 [29] He went up on a mountain and sat there, [30] and large crowds came to him, including the lame, the blind, the crippled, those unable to speak, and many others. They put them at his feet, and he healed them. [31] So the crowd was amazed when they saw those unable to speak talking, the crippled restored, the lame walking, and the blind seeing, and they gave glory to the God of Israel.

Jesus told them He would be their Savior.

Some people believed Him.

25 Jesus said to her, "I am the resurrection and the life. The one who believes in me, even if he dies, will live. 26 Everyone who lives and believes in me will never die. Do you believe this?" 27 "Yes, Lord," she told him, "I believe you are the Messiah, the Son of God, who comes into the world."

John 11:25—27

John 12:37 ³⁷ Even though he had performed so many signs in their presence, they did not believe in him.

They arrested Jesus and
sent Him to die.

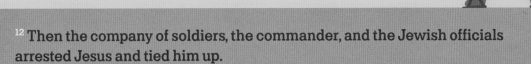

[12] Then the company of soldiers, the commander, and the Jewish officials arrested Jesus and tied him up.

John 18:12

Jesus
gave His life
on the cross.

He took the punishment
for our sin.

1 Peter 2:24   ²⁴ He himself bore our sins in his body on the tree; so that, having died to sins, we might live for righteousness. By his wounds you have been healed.

Our punishment should be

death
& separation

from God.

But Jesus
died for us.

¹⁶ For God loved the world in this way: He gave his one and only Son, so that everyone who believes in him will not perish but have eternal life.

John 3:16

Jesus was buried in a tomb.

Matthew 27:66   [66] They went and secured the tomb by setting a seal on the stone and placing the guard.

But after three days, He rose from the dead.

Jesus defeated sin and death!

[6] "Don't be alarmed," he said. "You are looking for Jesus of Nazareth, who was crucified. He has risen! He is not here."

Mark 16:6

Because Jesus took our PUNISHMENT, we don't have to be SEPARATED from God anymore.

1 Peter 3:18   [18] For Christ also suffered for sins once for all, the righteous for the unrighteous, that he might bring you to God.

When we **believe** Jesus died in our place,

and we **ask** God to forgive our sin,

we are **saved.**

This is the
GOS

PEL.

After He rose from the dead,

Jesus promised His people
He would send them a Helper—

THE HOLY SPIRIT.

John 14:25-26

[25] I have spoken these things to you while I remain with you. [26] But the Counselor, the Holy Spirit, whom the Father will send in my name, will teach you all things and remind you of everything I have told you.

The Holy Spirit helps us believe in Jesus. This is the

GIFT OF FAITH.

[8] For you are saved by grace through faith, and this is not from yourselves; it is God's gift— [9] not from works, so that no one can boast.

Ephesians 2:8-9

FAMILY

When we have faith in Jesus,
we become part of God's family.

Galatians 3:26 26 For through faith you are all sons of God in Christ Jesus.

We belong to

GOD

FOREVER!

[38] For I am persuaded that neither death nor life, nor angels nor rulers, nor things present nor things to come, nor powers, [39] nor height nor depth, nor any other created thing will be able to separate us from the love of God that is in Christ Jesus our Lord.

Romans 8:38-39

Believing in Jesus changes the way we live.
The Holy Spirit makes us more like Jesus every day.

Colossians 3:12–14 [12] Therefore, as God's chosen ones, holy and dearly loved, put on compassion, kindness, humility, gentleness, and patience, [13] bearing with one another and forgiving one another if anyone has a grievance against another. Just as the Lord has forgiven you, so you are also to forgive. [14] Above all, put on love, which is the perfect bond of unity.

Jesus tells us to **share the** GOOD NEWS about His love with the whole world!

[19] Go, therefore, and make disciples of all nations, baptizing them in the name of the Father and of the Son and of the Holy Spirit, [20] teaching them to observe everything I have commanded you.

Matthew 28:19-20

One day, Jesus will come to earth again

and rule as

KING

over God's good creation.

Revelation 21:3 ³ Then I heard a loud voice from the throne: Look, God's dwelling is with humanity, and he will live with them. They will be his peoples, and God himself will be with them and will be their God.

He will make

EVERYTHING NEW.

There will be no more
**fighting,
disappointment,
sickness,
and death.**

[4] He will wipe away every tear from their eyes. Death will be no more; grief, crying, and pain will be no more, because the previous things have passed away. [5] Then the one seated on the throne said, "Look, I am making everything new."

Revelation 21:4–5

John 10:28 [28] I give them eternal life, and they will never perish. No one will snatch them out of my hand.

And we will

NEVER

be

SEPARATED

from God again!

[5] These words are faithful and true.   Revelation 21:5

As you read this book with your child, they may have questions. Here are some ways to talk to your child about what they've read:

✻ Ask them what they liked and didn't like about this story.

✻ Discuss the parts of the story that were unfamiliar to them.

✻ Ask them to retell the story in their own words.

✻ Reflect on the ways sin impacts your family, your community, and the world.

✻ Reflect on the ways the gospel impacts your family, your community, and the world.

Here are some next steps you can take together:

✻ Pray regularly as a family.

✻ Read the Bible together.

✻ If your child is ready to follow Jesus, invite them to pray and pray with them.

✻ Think about who you'd like to share the gospel with. Pray for them together.

A Note to Parents

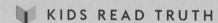 KIDS READ TRUTH

Kids Read Truth is a companion to
She Reads Truth and He Reads Truth.

STOP BY
kidsreadtruth.com

SHOP
shopkidsreadtruth.com

KEEP IN TOUCH
@kidsreadtruth

SEND A NOTE
hello@shereadstruth.com

SHARE
#KidsReadTruth